CHAOS IN PARADISE

Paradise Dickinson

BookLeaf
Publishing

India | USA | UK

Presentation by *BookLeaf Publishing*

Web: www.bookleafpub.com

E-mail: info@bookleafpub.com

ISBN: 9789363315266

First edition 2024

This book is dedicated to anyone who struggles with self-love, worth, and acceptance. To those who have suffered domestic violence and/or sexual assault; to anyone who has struggled with any kind of abuse. This book is for those of you who feel lost, alone, cold and dark. This is for YOU! You no longer need to "stay quiet."

SPEAK UP!
SPEAK OUT!
USE YOUR VOICE!
SET YOURSELF FREE!

ACKNOWLEDGEMENT

To my ancestors before me: without you all uniquely guiding, helping, strengthening, conditioning, preparing, teaching, and loving me, I would not be where I am today. I would not be able to help others overcome their struggles.

PREFACE

Before flipping the page, please make sure you are in a safe space and have a clear mind. This work has the potential to bring up triggers and unhealed traumas that you have stored inside your mind, body, heart, and soul. My intention in writing this book is to make people aware of their surroundings, thoughts, and feelings. I want you to know that you are not alone in whatever trials you are facing. You never have been, and you never will be.

one.

red, orange, and yellow flames burst so brightly.
a hot golden flake just hit the paper lightly.
flames everywhere.
run. don't panic. don't scream.
grab the keys. don't forget the dog.
is everyone out?

two.

kinda cliché really.
more of what you dreamt.
you see if you take a moment and slow down.
fucking breathe.
those really take the hit.
this place is nonexistent.
well-kept. secluded.
secret spot.

three.

chest feeling tight.
i just got into a fight.
battles that you must face on the inside.
between your souls' ties.
they say it's all in your mind.

four.

crash, burn, fall.
hurricane season.
soul-ties.

five.

hug everyone.
333 strangers.
30 seconds each
oxytocin.
boost immune system.
relieve some stress.
that's love.
i am love.

six

see it all.
feel it all.
everything and everyone.
loving is the only way of living.
carry your light.
love everyone right.
living is all about loving.

seven

it's hot.
surrounded by rock.
quiet. destination.
listening to the waves.
dark walk.

eight.

sitting in silence.
listening to gaia for divine guidance.
commotion in my head.

nine.

9

paired with the moon.
flowers bloom.
plentiful. grateful.
one day.
either way.

ten.

flowers.
red, orange, yellow petals spreading open into
the world.
blue, purple, and gold, more petals start to
unfold.
magical powers.
magical flowers.

eleven.

staring at the ocean's view.
turning my head to see the ghost of you.
as if i am dead, but i know i am not—
i am alive.
dead on the inside.

twelve.

they are the problem.
the problem is me.
mistakes.
lack of actions.

thirteen.

uproot your whole life.
for better. for worse.
wedding vows.

fourteen.

close once.
damn.
only experience, destruction.

fifteen.

firm believer, it's never for the better or for the
worse.
you cannot combine the two.
it's better, or it's worse.
nothing else.
i got the worst.

sixteen.

piece of shit.
little bitch.
you aren't shit.
abusive prick.

seventeen.

at this point, i don't even think you were ever
even sober.
coke, marijuana, and alcohol; the combination of
it all.

eighteen.

thriving in the darkest times.
i am a warrior.
grateful.
thorn hits in the chest—
breathe.

nineteen.

vortex. home.
tournament.
chose me though.
start to feel alive.

twenty.

my heart still ticks for you.
day in and day out.
beating and thumping and beating some more.
and truthfully, i don't want it to ever stop.
tick-tock. tick-tock.
not like my grandfather's clock.
then i would need the key.
to change out the battery.
but you see, i gave you that key when you first
met me.
thump-thump. thump-thump.
your heart's on borrowed time, but hell, so is
mine.
yours literal time. i think i need to sit down and
have a glass of red wine.
they say it's good for the heart, just one glass a
day. filled with antioxidants, resveratrol so they
say.
not for a weak heart. not yours anyway.
scared to imagine one day having to lay you at
your feet.
if we could just reverse-it-all, i'd give you the
best. i'd make sure to pass all your tests.
tick-tock-tick-tock-tick-tock.
my heart still ticks for you.
day in and day out.

twenty-one.

staring out the window.
been a couple years.
may showers, forget about all the flowers.
tears would once absorb into the ground.
silent, without making any sound.
may showers, there are no beautiful flowers.
colorful. wonderful. deep-rooted.
strong.

twenty-two.

gifted you kunzite.
will i ever forget about you?
months have gone by, so you haven't gotten to
tell me any of your lies.
fifteen past three, i bet you're up right now
thinking about me.
i mean i would be too, had i not forgotten all
about you.
but remember this.
i wasn't worth your time, so now you aren't
getting mine.

twenty-three.

knock. knock. who's there?
are you busy right now? i just happened to be on
your side of the town.
my side of the town?
you're a little mouse, coming and going just as
you please.

twenty-four.

my last thought of you and a memory that will
fade into the blue.
you don't love me, but stay for a little while.

twenty-five.

you've done a lot, have you not?
when i needed you most, you went completely
ghost.
nice toy on the shelf, you bought it so i could
play with it all by myself.
you've done a lot, have you not?
okay, well what about when i was being
touched? man, now that was tough.
i told you several times, but you insisted all i
was doing was telling lies.
you've done a lot, have you not?
well, what about when my period started?
it was like you just upped, disappeared and
darted.
blood seeping down my legs, on one of my
sisters' birthdays.
you've done a lot, have you not?
despite the lack of proper care for me growing
up.
never protected me in the night.
at least i can say that it made me extremely
tough.
'cause my childhood was completely rough.

twenty-six.

you left my heart broken.
like the gate in my neighbor's driveway.
dragging me around for a whole year.
until i decided to move back home and
disappear.
you came to open me right up, only to force me
closed again.

twenty-seven.

bought the supplies to mend it all back together.
hammer, nails, screws.
my heart, that is.
left completely broken.
i am unbreakable now.

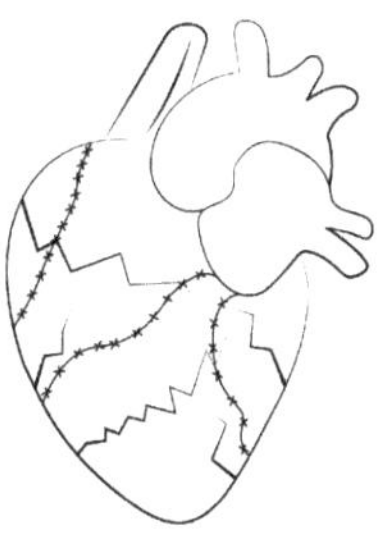

twenty-eight.

molestation went on for decades and
generations.
had to get a doctor and therapist evaluation.
retained lots of information—
it wasn't from a college education.
lost my identification.
most of my communication.
because of the situation.
moved across the country,
to build a better foundation.
for the kids and ongoing generations.

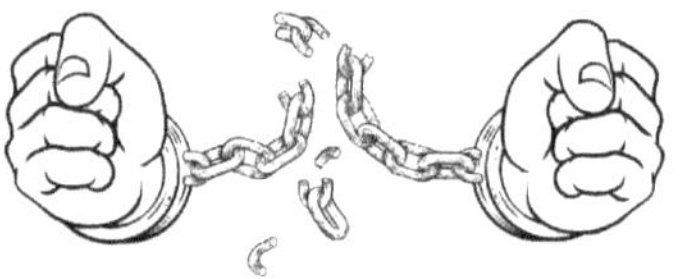

twenty-nine.

29

they say love is a choice, but i don't believe that
to be true.
because if that was the case, then why do i keep
loving all of you?
i may love myself, but i really love him, her,
them, they, and you too.
love is a choice—yet i will always love you.

thirty.

i am heavily protected because i make sure to
always stay connected.
i am divinely guided so there is no hiding.
i am grounded, safe, and secure at every turn.
i am worthy and loved, may i come give you and
your friends a hug?
after all is said and done, let's have some fun!

thirty-one

she wakes up and prays, thanks herself for a
brand-new day.
but before she lays down at night, she makes
sure she is alright.
she forgives herself for her sins.
she's always going to be her own friend.
she knows when she is wrong.
she knows when she is right.
she knows how to put up a fight.
she's going to stand up for what is right, even on
the darkest of nights.
she's going to stand up for all the people because
we are all equal.
fight for our beliefs and pray for world peace.
remember we are equal; we are here for the
people.

thirty-two.

this world is so full of hate, this isn't up for any
debate.
debating is part of the cause of why the world is
going to fall.
we all have our own fate, even a set expiration
date.
why waste our light if we are all meant to shine
bright?
stand up! come join me in the fight.
it is our divine birthright.

thirty-three.

your love is like the solar flares of the sun.
bright. blinding. unexpected and hot.
it's like hearing the soothing sounds of the birds
chirping on a cold, snowy, wintery day.
even with the snow dripping away.
your love is like the ocean, rushing up to the
shoreline and pulling me back in, so close to
you.
it's like connecting the freckles on your body to
make starry constellations, as if i am already
gazing up at
the stars—because you are a star.
your love is like the calm in the eye of the storm.
your love is like looking into your eyes and
seeing the world slowly fade away.
it's like watching the full moon light up the night
sky to guide me back home to you.
your love is pure, magnetic, and true.
that is partly why i love you.

thirty-four.

don't ever want to know what it feels like to be
pushed down.
he loves you, so you let him.
don't ever want to know what it feels like to be
slapped.
he loves you, so you let him.
don't ever want to be told to change the way you
look.
he loves you, so you do.
don't ever want to know what it feels like to be
punched.
he loves you, so you let him.
don't ever want to know what it feels like for
your body to crash through the living room wall,
watch all your family photos fly off and fall.
he loves you, so you let him.
don't ever want to know what it feels like to
have a freshly new set of acrylic nails ripped off.
but he loves you, so you let him.
don't ever want to know what it feels like to
have your head clash against the pavement.
he loves you, so you let him.
don't ever want to feel the weight of a trailblazer
run your ankle over.
he loves you, so you let him.

you stop, catch a breath and think, *"is this what love is?"*
you slowly realize he's never loved you.
you realize it should've never happened.
instead, you let it because you loved him.
the only love you've ever received was chaos
and never the actual dream.
the power of love can be confusing and
deceiving if you never knew what love truly was
from the beginning.

thirty-five.

want to know what it feels like to slow-dance
with no music playing.
the sounds of the trees swaying, the wind
whistling,
while the birds are chirping, or the frogs are
ribbiting.
want to know what it feels like to come home
after a long day and hear the words,
"how was your day?" "are you okay?"
want to know what it feels like to be able to cry
and be held.
at the same damn time.
want to know what it feels like to laugh until
you can no longer bear to breathe.
want to know what it feels like to have your hair
played with without asking.
have a hand running down your spine without
questioning and getting anxiety.
feel warm skin pressed against yours all through
the night.
want to have intellectual conversations around
midnight.
our futures, dreams, hopes, desires, and goals.
the stars, the galaxy, the afterlife, and growing
old.
feel welcomed, accepted, and loved.

want to know what it feels like to feel.
want to know if being loved by someone else is
even real.

thirty-six.

dear god, i kneel before you today to give you
thanks for attempting to keep all this chaos at
bay.
you've done a phenomenal job even though i
still feel robbed.
i feel robbed of my innocence and of my peace,
it is still so hard to sometimes sleep.
i thank you today, tomorrow, and more days to
come for everything that you have ever done.
i know you have a plan; i promise i will get to it
soon, but first i must talk to selene, the moon.
i need to be patient, keep faith and the
lighthouse glowing.
the ocean seems to keep fighting against me.
with all the commotion, it has such devotion.
you've helped me sail through the storm.

thirty-seven.

hot and rough on the outside but warm, red, and
soft on the inside.
gladly take the knife and stab so hard, the juice
squirts out.
splashing in my face, grinning with joy.
liquid drips, falling back into the puddle
beneath.
licking my lips, taking the knife twice more to
slice again.
couple pieces so i can watch it ooze as i pull
apart.
the inside looks just like i imagined.
red. warm. soft.
except, it looks better than i imagined.
red. warm. soft. extra juicy.
who knew there could be so much inside.
the puddle beneath is bigger now.
kept stabbing and slicing into pieces.
section by section, little by little, until it's all cut
up and there's nothing left to dig into.
until the puddle is overflowing and making a
mess.
take my fork and start eating.
savoring every bite, feeling the juice squirt late
at night.
so juicy and delicious.

just like that, gone.
on to the next with a smile on my face.

40

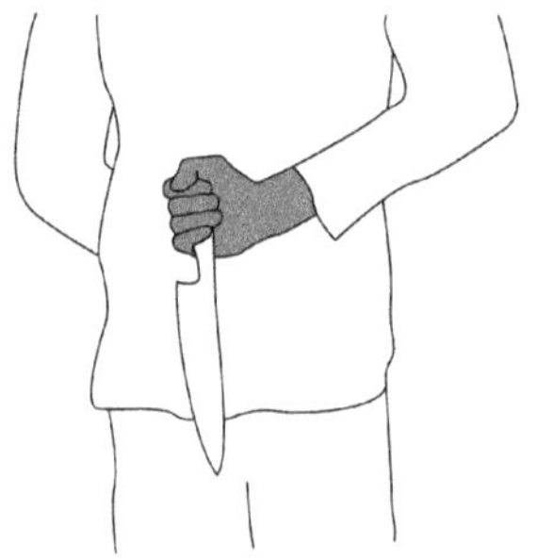

thirty-eight.

little p, you are always safe with me.
there is no need to be scared now—
come out and play.
little p, you are always free to speak.
we hear you now, more than ever before.
i promise i will never close the door.
it's an open-door policy around here.
little p, you are loved like a sweet honeybee.
you are wild and you are free.
flying from wildflower to wildflower.
wild like the wind and the leaves of the oak
trees.
it's time to pollinate and grow—it's your hour.
you are smart, kind, and wonderfully beautiful.
your light always shines across the entire sky.
shines like the sun, beams like the moon.
even on the dark days that you think are gloomy.
little p, i promise you are always safe with me.
don't be scared now, come take my hand.
i will never leave your side; i am here for the
entire ride.

thirty-nine.

to be loved without being afraid,
that it's all going to fade.
love someone who will reciprocate,
the same energy and level of love that you give.
bleeding out of your soul like it's your last
lifeline to this life of yours.

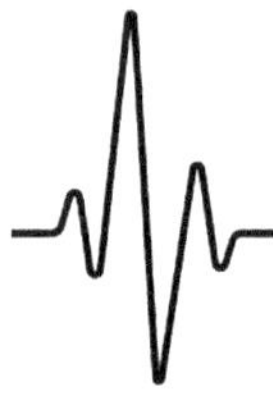

forty.

what if breathing is the very last thing i want to
do,
after staying up all night and talking with selene,
the moon.

forty-one.

i am a house plant with complex emotions.
sunlight. water. food. repeat.

forty-two.

sometimes i just want to be numb.
then there are moments where i am just lying
with my eyes closed,
listening in silence, and my mind goes quiet.
feeling the feeling of my eyelids tingling,
imagine if i was numb.
how then, i would not feel my eyes.
thinking if i can not feel them, then i cannot feel
my body.

forty-three.

he was playing the game,
i was tired of competing.

forty-four.

47

baby, crying.
sirens, whining.
screams from down the street.
nothing left to eat.

forty-five.

he hit me,
beaten and abused.
told me he never would.
told myself i'd leave,
the next time i could.
never left before, always stayed.
not this time, he hit me.

forty-six.

tired eyes.
tired heart.
she has risen from the dark.

forty-seven.

hyper-fixations seem to be the only equation.
no acquaintances, just my brain.

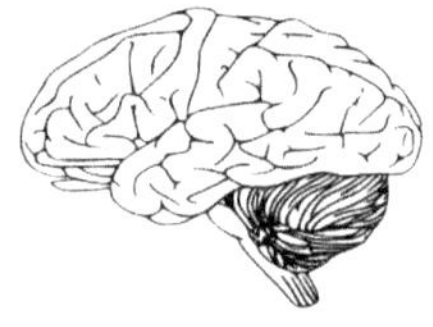

forty-eight.

blood in veins,
in my mind.
blood in heart,
in my lungs.
i am drowning.

forty-nine.

52

target on my back,
shell blocking all the hits.
it is just a matter of time before it cracks.

fifty.

they told me they would tell me when they're
proud.
i am still waiting.

fifty-one.

locking myself away from the world.
so, i can disappear in my own madness.

fifty-two.

55

death comes to visit me often.
tells me he's just checking in.
he offers me a way out.
i told him i was not ready.
come back later.

fifty-three.

56

i lay there rocking until the river flowed.
too tired to move, so i sunk to the bottom.

fifty-four.

my mind stayed young,
while my body grew old.
my heart stopped beating,
they were told.

fifty-five.

it is not a dream,
but somehow no one could hear my screams.
right next door, i was just being ignored.

fifty-six.

cannot fathom another lie.
cannot just sit down in silence.
cannot deny.

fifty-seven.

bees are buzzing around,
dandelions sporadically on the ground.
chrysanthemums growing in the pots,
worms wiggling under the rocks.

fifty-eight.

61

like the roots of the oak trees connecting to each
other
i grasp onto myself, pulling me back together.
taking all that i have, in hopes that
it does not turn out the same as before.

fifty-nine.

62

death comes.
sweeping away what no longer belongs.
grasping onto the souls of the wrong.
feeding the night's delight.

sixty.

loyal. patient. kind.
loving. passionate. understanding.
honest and compassionate too.
gives me space when it's needed,
so that i do not get depleted.

sixty-one.

chaos, i can hardly breathe.
wrestling with confusion, i am on my knees.
rinse, recycle, and repeat.
i've got nothing left inside of me.

sixty-two.

empty on the inside
contradictions every day.
souls floating.
exhausted. haunted.

sixty-three.

emotions hitting,
distorting reality.
scared. questions.
never-ending.

sixty-four.

67

holding a candle in the dark,
waiting for it to burn out.
dark once more, then light.

sixty-five.

laughing was simpler, easier, and a hundred
times more frequent then.
now, i am just a blue butterfly being chased by a
lion without water.
what seems to be around the clock.
head in the clouds, fork in the road, too many
ways to go.
lost looking for the gem.

sixty-six.

69

mother abused me, used me.
never listened or showed real love.
father abused me, used me.
never listened or showed real love.
mother. father.

sixty-seven.

freedom, at last.
running wild with the wolves.
howling from the mountains,
gazing upon the stars.
falling back into a state of bliss.
freedom, at last.

sixty-eight.

overcoming, one-of-a-kind soul.
self-growth journey, own constant companion.
leaving a lasting imprint of success.
embarked on.

sixty-nine.

immersing myself into the dark deep blue ocean,
riding the sea urchins across the cold sand.
immersing my body deep into the land.
so warm and gold.

seventy.

in the bed of oak roots, still giving life after i am
gone.
nourishing and caring for othcrs, giving back to
the earth where i once walked.
feeling life growing from the inside as you once
did time and time again.
everlasting eternal love.

seventy-one.

74

planting seeds for flowers to grow.
scorpion grasses, daffodils, lavender and more.
wildflowers fields for everyone to adore.
locked greenhouse for the poison plants too.
just to sit and admire in my brain what i'd do to
you.